Michael Rear

GW00374816

BLESSED JOHN HENRY NEWMAN

ST PAULS

First published in 1983 by the Incorporated Catholic Truth Society
and The Church Literature Association.
Revised 2010.

Cover image: John Henry Newman (1868). A portrait by A.R. Venables.
Used with the permission of Oxford Oratory.

ST PAULS Publishing
187 Battersea Bridge Road, London, SW11 3AS, UK
www.stpaulpublishing.com

ISBN 978-085439-789-1

Typeset by MIDDLEDOT, London, UK

Printed and bound in the UK by Intype Libra Ltd
Wimbledon, London

ST PAULS is an activity of the priests and brothers of the Society
of St Paul who proclaim the Gospel through the media of social
communication.

Contents

OXFORD   **6**

Friends   *6*

The Oxford Movement   *14*

The Development of Doctrine   *20*

ROME   **25**

The Oratorians   *25*

Education   *27*

On Consulting the Faithful   *28*

The First Vatican Council   *31*

Conscience   *32*

A Cardinal   *37*

Blessed are the Meek   *41*

TWO PRAYERS OF CARDINAL NEWMAN   **47**

JOHN HENRY NEWMAN, theologian, pastor, teacher, writer and cardinal: his life spanned most of the nineteenth century, yet he was called a man for the twentieth. No one influenced the Church of England more than he during his lifetime; few have influenced the Roman Catholic Church more since his death, and he continues to do so. His long life (1801-1890) was spent almost equally in both Churches. The eldest son of a happy marriage between a London banker and a woman of French Huguenot descent, John Henry was brought up in an undistinguished but gentle Anglican household, where the Bible and Catechism were read and the way of Christian living firmly implanted. At the age of fifteen he experienced, through the guidance of an Anglican evangelical clergyman, Walter Mayers ('the human means of the beginning of divine faith in me,' Newman wrote), an 'inward conversion' about which, even in his sixty-third year, he was able to confess, 'I still am more certain than that I have hands and feet.'

Nevertheless, the conversion was tainted with the Calvinist 'detestable doctrine' (as he later called it) that the elect are incapable of falling away, that the converted and the unconverted can be discriminated by man, and that the justified are conscious of their state of justification. Like many evangelicals his outlook was formed by a particular view of Scriptural authority which gave no place for the Church; altogether lacking a sense of the history and continuity of the Church, he was led into a hostile attitude against the Roman

Catholic Church, convinced that the Pope was the anti-Christ. Such robust hostility is not easily dislodged.

> My imagination was stained by the effects of this doctrine up to the year 1843; it had been obliterated from my reason and judgment at an earlier date; but the thought remained upon me as a sort of false conscience.[1]

Many others have experienced a similar antipathy and will sense exactly what Newman meant.

OXFORD

Friends

The highly intelligent young man of sixteen went up to Trinity College, Oxford. Through nervous anxiety he spoilt his finals, quickly retrieving the disaster by winning a prestigious Fellowship to Oriel College in 1822. Fellows were expected to be ordained, a stipulation that did little to adorn the priesthood, but for Newman there was a true vocation within. On 13 June 1824 he was ordained Deacon, and wrote in his journal:

> It is over. I am thine, Lord ... At first, after the hands were laid on me, my heart shuddered within me; the words 'for ever' are so terrible ... At times indeed my heart burned within me, particularly during the singing of the *Veni Creator*. Yet Lord, I ask not for comfort in comparison with sanctification.[2]

1   John Henry Newman, *Apologia Pro Vita Sua,* Fontana, 1959, Part III, p. 100.
2   Cited in, Charles Stephen Dessain, *John Henry Newman*, Nelson, 1966, p. 7.

Next day he wrote, 'I have a responsibility of souls on me to the day of my death.' He truly meant this, and everything he did in his life, from preaching and teaching to writing his celebrated books, in all the controversies that ensued, this was his one end, the salvation of souls. It was in a poor parish, St Clement's, just outside Oxford, that he took up this responsibility as a curate and prepared for the priesthood. Visiting his flock house by house, getting to know and loving each person, he began to lose that hard, unreal distinction between the saved and the damned. Crowds who came to hear him preach had to be turned away from the doors, and for two happy years he laboured in this parish, until at Easter 1826 he was made tutor of his college.

At about the same time, Richard Hurrell Froude, as ardent a catholic-minded Anglican as Newman was evangelical, was also appointed tutor; churchmanship kept them apart, and it was more than a year before they became close friends. After that no one had more influence on Newman than he. One of the few Anglicans of the period to have a genuine understanding of the Church of Rome, he just could not believe Newman held it to be anti-Christian, and he it was who caused him to revise his ideas.

> I speak of Hurrell Froude, in his intellectual aspect, as a man of high genius, brimful and overflowing with ideas and views ... He had an intellect as critical and logical as it was

speculative and bold … It is difficult to enumerate the precise additions to my theological creed which I derived from a friend to whom I owe so much. He made me look with admiration towards the Church of Rome, and in the same degree to dislike the Reformation. He fixed deep in me the idea of devotion to the Blessed Virgin, and he led me gradually to believe in the Real Presence.[3]

In Oriel College Common Room, a Movement, later to be known as the *Oxford Movement*, was stirring. When Froude died young in 1836 Newman lost a dear friend indeed, but there were others. There was Edward Bouverie Pusey, another Fellow of Oriel, who soon left Oxford to pursue his studies in Germany, before returning as Regius Professor of Hebrew. And there was John Keble.

Keble's had been the first name Newman had heard mentioned, not just with admiration but with reverence, soon after coming to Oxford. Although they overlapped only by a year, they were destined to become close friends when Keble came back as Professor of Poetry eight years later. Keble's collection of poetry, *The Christian Year,* published in 1827, contained teaching Newman called 'so deep, so pure, so beautiful' it awoke in him, as it did in the hearts of thousands, a new appreciation of the mystery of the sacraments. Christians everywhere love to sing *Blest are the Pure in Heart*, perhaps the most famous poem in his collection. Keble led Newman to see how the intellectual grasp of truth is

---

3   *Apologia*, pp. 113-4.

appropriated by the imagination and heart into faith in one living, personal and present God. It is faith and love that give intellectual probability its certainty. Newman was to take Keble's idea much further in his later sermons and essays, and to its conclusion in *A Grammar of Assent*, published in his seventieth year, offered to show the educated agnostic how it is possible to believe what cannot be understood or absolutely proved. It is a theme to which he returned again and again; that doctrine, far from being merely a matter of the intellect, or dealing with abstractions, is the bearer of objective truths, which can be known with certitude and assented to with joy and ease. On this the spiritual life is built. We may hear an echo of Newman both in the First Vatican Council and in *Verbum Dei* at the Second, which speaks of the Holy Spirit moving the heart and opening the eyes of the mind, 'making it easy for all to accept and believe the truth.'

In 1828 Newman, as well as being a tutor at Oriel, was appointed Vicar of the University Church, St Mary's. Here he inaugurated Sunday afternoon sermons at 4 p.m., and these *Parochial and Plain Sermons*, were, he acknowledged, the source of his influence among townspeople, students, graduates and fellows, who packed the church to hear him for the next fifteen years. He preached often of sanctification, but he also called for conversion:

> When a man comes to God to be saved, then, I say, the

essence of true conversion is a surrender of himself, an unreserved, unconditional surrender ... . What is it that we who profess religion lack? I repeat it, this: a willingness to be changed, a willingness to suffer (if I may use such a word), to suffer Almighty God to change us. We do not like to let go our old selves.[4]

He spoke frequently of the unseen world, and of our living in it:

It is then the duty and privilege of all disciples of our glorified Saviour, to be exalted and transfigured with Him; to live in heaven in their thoughts, motives, aims, desires, likings, prayers, praises, intercessions, even while they are in the flesh; to look like other men, to be busy like other men, to be passed over in the crowd of men or even to be scorned or oppressed, as other men may be, but the while to have a secret channel of communication with the Most High, a gift the world knows not of; to have their life hid with Christ in God.[5]

Constantly speaking of the indwelling of the Holy Trinity, his words converted and inspired.

A true Christian, then, may almost be defined as one who has a ruling sense of God's Presence with him. As none but the justified persons have that privilege, so none but the justified have that practical perception of it ... In all circumstances, of joy or sorrow, hope or fear, let us aim at having Him in our inmost heart; let us have no secret apart from Him. Let us acknowledge Him as enthroned within us at the very springs of thought and affection ... this is the true life of saints. This is to have the Spirit witnessing with our spirits that we are sons of God.[6]

---

4   *Parochial and Plain Sermons V*, cited in Dessain, p. 59.
5   *Parochial and Plain Sermons VI*, cited in Dessain, p. 53.
6   *Parochial and Plain Sermons V*, cited in Dessain, p. 50.

He spoke quietly, read his sermons, used no gestures, but his words pierced the heart. The historian, James Anthony Froude, the brother of Hurrell, described a sermon in which Newman recounted closely some incidents in Our Lord's Passion.

> And then he paused. For a few moments there was a breathless silence. Then in a low clear voice, of which the faintest vibration was audible in the farthest corner of St Mary's, he said, 'Now I bid you consider that He to whom these things were done was Almighty God.' It was as if an electric stroke was gone through the church. As if every person present understood for the first time the meaning of what he had all his life been saying.[7]

The parish included the village of Littlemore, which lacked a church. This deficiency Newman soon remedied when his mother, who had come to live nearby, laid the foundation stone of a charming church. But the newly-appointed Provost of Oriel, Edward Hawkins, whom Newman had succeeded as Vicar of St Mary's, began to resent Newman's influence in College. Newman, Hurrell Froude, and another tutor, Robert Wilberforce (the son of the evangelical slave-liberator William Wilberforce), were giving private tutorials free of charge as part of their normal teaching method, and had assumed not only an academic but also a pastoral role towards their undergraduates.

The latter was inherent in their understanding of

---

7   James Anthony Froude, *Short Studies of Great Subjects*, vol. 4, Longmans, Green & Co., London, 1899, p. 286.

education. In the history of his religious opinions he called *Apologia Pro Vita Sua*, written in response to a terrible attack on him by Charles Kingsley, Newman describes a turning point in his brilliantly successful life as a young Oxford don, when he realised the dangers of fashionable rationalism: 'I was beginning to prefer intellectual excellence to moral; I was drifting in the direction of the Liberalism of the day.' Newman later developed his theories of education in *The Idea of a University*. University education is for the 'enlargement of mind', not the narrow training for a profession. No one appreciated the intellect more than Newman, but

> knowledge is one thing, virtue is another ... Philosophy, however enlightened, however profound, gives no command over the passions, no influential motives, no vivifying principles ... Quarry the granite rock with razors, or moor the vessel with a thread of silk; then may you hope with such keen and delicate instruments as human knowledge and human reason to contend against those giants, the passion and the pride of man.[8]

Of course, he was not anti-rational, believing that Reason, rightly exercised, leads the mind to the truth, but 'Reason, considered as a real agent in the world ... is far from taking so straight ... a direction.' In fact it is often characterised by 'scepticism of the intellect.' Pointing the finger at London University where religion and secular knowledge were separated like 'a sort of bazaar, or pantechnicon, in which wares of all kinds are heaped together for sale in stalls independent of each

---

8   John Henry Newman, *The Idea of a University*, Regnery Publications, 1999, p. 110.

other', he argues for a sense of unity in which 'learned men' view different disciplines as a whole and create 'a pure and clear atmosphere of thought, which the student also shares', and which necessarily includes theology. He is looking back at the original medieval idea of universities like Oxford and Cambridge, Paris, Bologna and Salamanca, 'the education of the whole man'. The tutorial system, pioneered for a pastoral purpose by Newman and the others, is commonplace in many universities today, but in 1830 Newman was forced by the Provost to resign. However, God often uses disappointments like this for his own purposes, and just at the right time Newman was approached by a publisher to write a book on the early Councils of the Church.

His former students presented him with volumes of the Fathers, those Christian theologians, some contemporary with the New Testament writers and others following them, with whose help, Newman had come to believe, the New Testament should be interpreted for its earliest, apostolic meaning. Such a way of discovering Christian doctrine in the New Testament differed sharply from that of evangelicals who treated the Bible as if it was a source book of texts to be interpreted without regard for the history and life of the Church in which it was inspired and written. Like many of the other Oxford Movement leaders, especially Dr Pusey, the chief editor of the *Library of the Fathers,* Newman became an authority on the Fathers. In years to come he reflected:

> In truth, this fidelity of the ancient Christian system, seen in modern Rome, was the luminous fact which more than any other turned men's minds at Oxford forty years ago to look towards her with reverence, interest and love. It affected individual minds variously of course: some it eventually brought on to conversion, others it only restrained from active opposition to her claims; but none of us could read the Fathers, and determine to be their disciples, without feeling that Rome, like a faithful steward, had kept in fullness and vigour what our own communion had let drop.[9]

One of the most charming books Newman wrote was a novel, *Callista,* composed in his mellifluous style; meticulously researched, it tells the story of the third century Christian Church in North Africa, vividly picturing its life, to show what early Christianity was really like. It was written in 1855, but that is to leap ahead.

The Oxford Movement

The Oxford Movement began, Newman always said, with a sermon preached by Keble. It was on 14 July 1833 in St Mary's Church before the Judges of Assize; his subject, *National Apostasy*, defending the Church of England against the proposed suppression by the government of ten bishoprics in Ireland. He called on the State and its leaders to return to God from apostasy, and to respect the Church and its bishops, the successors of the apostles. The reaction to

9   John Henry Newman, *Letter to the Duke of Norfolk*, Sufi Press, 2008, p. 20

his sermon convinced these Oxford friends of the influence they could have if they tried. The Oxford Movement had been conceived, years of discussions in Oriel College were coming to fruition, and Keble, in St Mary's pulpit, signalled its birth. Newman and Froude had spent the previous months in the Mediterranean where Newman had been taken seriously ill and where he had written his moving poem *Lead kindly light*, which became a much loved hymn. It expressed so well Newman's desire always to trust in God's guidance and presence, to let not pride rule his will, and be content for God to show him the way, 'one step enough for me.' And so the Oxford Movement began.

The nineteenth century way to proceed was by tracts. September 1833 saw the issuing of *Tracts for the Times*; first off the press a four-page penny pamphlet by Newman on the apostolic succession entitled, *Thoughts on the Ministerial Commission, respectfully addressed to the Clergy.* Within a year forty-seven anonymous tracts had been published, mostly written by Newman, others by Keble, Froude and a layman, John Bowden. One of them, on fasting, was written by Pusey, which he boldly signed with his initials to signify his formal adhesion to the Movement. Around and about Oxford, from parsonage to parsonage, rode Newman and his friends on horseback distributing bundles of tracts, which were eagerly sought and bought. The pamphlets spread far. Meetings assembled, gatherings, dinners, soirées, and a voluminous correspondence ensued, Newman reinforcing it all by packing St Mary's for his brilliant Parochial Sermons.

Despite the fact that certain tracts contained attacks on Rome ('their Communion is infected with heresy: we are bound to flee it as a pestilence' – Tract 20) the pamphlets were denounced as 'popery'. What they really sought to do, and in many ways succeeded in doing, was to revive within the Church of England a deeper understanding of the nature of the Church, its worship and its discipline.

To appreciate the enormous impact of the tracts it is necessary to know what the state of the Church of England was in those days More than half the clergy resided outside their parishes in 'better parts'. Families sent their sons 'into the Church', to be ordained because they could do nothing else. With few exceptions bishops were indolent and wealthy, hardly ever visiting their parishes or administering Confirmation. The Bishop of Winchester, for example, was said to have an income of £50,000 a year, while curates were paid £60 a year or less by incumbents made rich through holding livings in plurality. One Bishop of Llandaff hardly ever set foot in the diocese he ruled for over twenty years, proudly spending his time as an agriculturalist in the Lake District. A Bishop of Bristol had his palace burned down by a mob. Nor are these isolated instances, for although there certainly were some devout and industrious clergy, particularly among the evangelicals, the abuses of pluralism, non-residence, nepotism and sinecures had all flourished almost without interruption since before the Reformation. An Act against pluralism passed in the reign of Henry VIII had been completely ineffective. The Roman Catholic Church on the continent had confronted the same abuses by means of the Council of Trent (1545-1563) with marked success and a flood of missionary enterprise. Seminaries were established to educate the clergy and inspire their sense of vocation. But the Church of England had to wait three centuries for the Oxford Movement to do these things, and in his very first tract Newman tried to raise the spiritual vision of the clergy.

With such pastors, the Church of England was inevitably in poor shape. On Easter Day 1800 there were but six communicants in St Paul's Cathedral, London. Some other cathedrals were nearly in ruins and it was even proposed by one speaker at a public meeting that Canterbury Cathedral should be given over to the local cavalry for stables A few parish churches were well-attended, especially in the towns. Holy Communion was normally celebrated four or five times a year. The sick could not be anointed and confession had died out. Services were dreary and strangers to joy, though the singing of hymns was becoming more popular among evangelicals.

The Reformation had abolished religious communities and little or no social work was done for the poor. Pew rents effectively kept away the poor who, if they wanted to worship anywhere, were drawn to the chapel. Until Newman and his friends began to inspire holiness and revive the religious communities only the evangelicals, the Roman Catholics, and the non-conformists were making efforts to preach conversion and holiness, and to assist the poor.

Newman and the Tractarians were determined to prove that the Church, far from being just a department of State, as many saw it, was a divine institution founded by Christ himself. Its authority was not given to it by the State but had been handed down from generation to generation to the present-day bishops from the apostles, whose successors they were, though they scarcely realised it, or lived like it.

The *Tracts for the Times* fell like sparks on the dry tinder of the Church. Their effect was tremendous and the support nationwide. So was the opposition. Criticism of them reached fever pitch in 1841 when the ninetieth tract was published. Here, following the line of a seventeenth century Roman Catholic Franciscan, Christopher Davenport, it was asserted that the Thirty-Nine Articles of the Church of England are not contrary to Roman Catholic doctrine. They were aimed at corrupt Roman practices rather than doctrine, and were consequently capable of a Catholic interpretation not at variance with the Council of Trent. Hoping thereby to stem the tide of Anglicans beginning to 'go over to Rome' the tract reasoned that all things necessary could be found within the Church of England, including seven sacraments, the Real Presence of the Eucharist, a proper doctrine of purgatory, and the invocation of saints.

The reaction to Tract 90 was sensational, unbelievable. The whole body of protestant England rose up in fury. No one doubted that Newman was the author, though in truth Keble had pressed him to publish it. A violent torrent of anger was hurled at Newman. The Heads of the Oxford Colleges raged in opposition, and declared the tract incompatible with the University Statutes: his university career was ended. The Bishop of Oxford banned the publication of further tracts.

The effect on Newman was catastrophic and appalling. 'In every part of the country and every class of society, in newspapers, in pulpits, at dinner-tables, in coffee-rooms, in railway carriages, I was denounced as a traitor.' Needing to consider his future, and virtually driven from the Church of England by public opinion and hostile bishops, he slipped into exile at Littlemore with a small community of followers. In September 1843 he resigned his living of St Mary's, and preached in Littlemore Church his last sermon, which he called 'The Parting of Friends'. He continued to live at Littlemore, spending four and a half hours each day in prayer, nine more in translating the treatises of St Athanasius against Arius, gradually drawing the conclusion that as regards schism protestants were in a position similar to the Arians, while the *via media* of Anglicanism resembled the situation of the semi-Arians.

The Development of Doctrine

For more than four years at Littlemore Newman struggled with his opinion that Roman Catholics had added to the revealed truths that are found in Scripture. Such a man of integrity and intellect could not take one step towards the Catholic Church with this massive difficulty unresolved. Tentatively he began his *Essay on the Development of Doctrine.*

If St Athanasius or St Ambrose suddenly came to life it could not be doubted which communion they would recognise as their own. Not that the Roman Catholic Church of the nineteenth century was the same in every respect as the Church of early centuries any more than the man is the same as the boy, but it was clearly the same body, the same living community, continuously developing in history. He concluded that the question of development turned on the nature of the promise of the Holy Spirit and the unity of the Church. He became more convinced that the Church of England was in schism than that Roman Catholic developments were not true ones, and delineated seven tests for distinguishing true developments from corruptions The Roman Catholic Church, he found, was not corrupt in any real sense:

> When a system really is corrupt, powerful agents, when applied to it, do but develop that corruption, and bring it more speedily to an end … Very different has been the history of Catholicism … It has borne, and can bear, principles and doctrines, which in other systems of religion quickly degenerate into fanaticism and infidelity.[10]

It was the end of the 'branch theory' by which Tractarians had maintained that the Catholic Church had divided into three branches, Roman, Orthodox and Anglican. For Newman, now, the Church had no branches. All antiquity bore witness to the unity of the Church. Doctrine develops, granted the assumption that Divine Providence was guiding the Church, giving it the capacity for renewal. Doctrines about the Mother of God, the Eucharist and the Papal Office were not to be seen as additions to the Gospel, but the outcome of the Church's collective pondering upon the Gospel of the Lord, just as in one sense the New Testament books themselves are. The Christian faith is not a list of revealed doctrinal articles, but 'a divine philosophy', a system of thought, for the Church possesses a kind of instinct, going back to the apostles and the Scriptures, for expressing the mind of Christ in its teaching.

Newman's teaching was so readily assimilated into Catholic theology (and part of the *Dogmatic Constitution on Divine Revelation* of the Second Vatican Council is practically a précis of his *Essay*), that it is not easy to grasp how revolutionary it was at the time. Protestants

---

10 John Henry Newman, *An Essay on the Development of Christian Doctrine*, Longmans, Green and Co., London, 1909, p. 443.

and Anglicans tended to see themselves as disciples of St Paul, immediate descendants of the New Testament, as though all theological writers after his day (except the Reformers) were irrelevant or corrupt. Catholics, too, sat lightly to history, in reliance on the teachings and systematic theology of the Church. In a few years' time Newman was to be shocked by the theology taught in the seminaries of Rome. 'There is an iron form here,' he wrote. It was a non-historical orthodoxy learnt from second-rate manuals. St Augustine was virtually unknown, and even St Thomas Aquinas was not read.

Newman was writing before Darwin (whose theory of evolution worried him not at all), and his unique contribution was to show how *ideas* develop as well as institutions. He looked on the Church as a continuous community of thought and theology as well as of love. It seems obvious to us today, and is the underlying assumption behind the Second Vatican Council's *Constitution on the Church*, in which the primary image of the Church is not that of an institution but of the pilgrim people of God, journeying in the history of the world.

It was long after Newman that what is often called 'Salvation History', the view that Christian Revelation is not a series of propositions but historical events revealing the living God, became taken seriously in both Anglican and Catholic teaching. His conclusion that Christianity as a universal religion develops different ways of relating to and dealing with the world, 'hence all bodies of Christians, orthodox or not, develop the doctrines of Scripture' has been called a handbook of missionary adaptation. It implies also that there must be a living authority in the Church, and the Fathers to whom he had continually appealed had been the very ones who witnessed to the existence of this authority.

Before the *Essay* was finished Newman saw his way clearly. On 9 October 1845, after writing a few letters to his sister and friends, Oxford's greatest son, the light of his generation, humbly asked a Passionist priest, Fr Dominic Barberi to hear his confession and receive him into what he had come to believe to be 'the one and only fold of the Redeemer'.

How Keble and Pusey, on whom now fell the mantle of leading the Oxford Movement, and many others, held together is a remarkable story. It grew with the years and transformed the face of the Church of England. In his obituary of Newman, in the *Guardian*, Dean Church of St Paul's Cathedral wrote, he 'was the founder, we may almost say, of the Church of England as we see it. What the Church of England would have become without the Tractarian movement we can faintly guess, and of the Tractarian movement Newman was the living soul and the inspiring genius.'[11] Daily Eucharists were restored, Religious Communities were revived, the practice of retreats and ways of prayer, and devotion to the Blessed

11 The Guardian, 13 August 1890.

23

Virgin Mary and the saints were fostered. In the face of fierce criticism and opposition to 'ritualism', priests eventually began to wear vestments and introduce pre-Reformation customs and ceremonies. Some adherents of the Movement pursued the goal of what they called 'corporate reunion' between the Church of England and the Roman Catholic Church. Newman thought that impossible. Yet, always he wrote in a gentle spirit, kept in touch with Pusey and others, and in his lectures on *The Difficulties of Anglicans* he told his audience that he had 'only pleasant associations of those many years when I was within her pale', reminding them nonetheless that the Church of England is a National Church and that 'nothing could make it Catholic again'. The continuing spread of Anglo-Catholicism was not inevitable and would be followed by the rise of liberalism, he thought.

So it was that hundreds of university and educated men, families, priests and laity followed Newman in the next few years. Pusey wrote most kindly after Newman's secession:

> Our Church has not known how to employ him. And since this was so, it seemed as if a sharp sword were lying in its scabbard … He seems to me not so much gone from us, as transplanted into another part of the vineyard, where the full energies of his powerful mind can be employed.[12]

---

12 Cited in Dessain, p. 85.

ROME

The Oratorians

Two of the Littlemore community had joined the Catholic Church a few days before Newman. The other two were received with him, and they moved as a group to a former college at Oscott near Birmingham, which had been kindly provided for their use. Within a year they went their separate ways to prepare for the priesthood. Newman and his companion, Ambrose St John, it was decided should go to Rome, and early in September 1846 they set off to study theology at the Propaganda College and discern their vocations. On 30 May 1847 Newman was ordained a Catholic priest.

Curiously enough it was partly the character of Keble that helped them decide what they would do next. For Keble reminded Newman of the great sixteenth century priest, St Philip Neri, who had founded communities of secular priests living together with 'no rule but that of love', in groups called 'Oratories'. When Newman left Rome in November 1847 after his Oratorian noviciate at *Santa Croce*, he had the Pope's authority to found Oratories in England. His intention was not to reproduce an exact copy of the Italian Oratories but to actuate St Philip's ideas in a different situation. The first Oratory was established in Birmingham, and Newman devoted himself to the people of the parish, to the children and the poor, many of them Irish, driven to England by the potato famine. Writing many years later,

Bishop William Ullathorne reminded Newman how in a cholera epidemic at Bilston he asked Newman whether he could spare two priests from the Oratory to assist two of his diocesan priests who were already working night and day. 'But you and Father St John preferred to take the place of danger, which I had destined for others, and remained at Bilston till the worst was over.'

It is difficult to overestimate what the Oratory meant to Newman. In it he planted his heart, he loved it, and made of it the framework for the rest of his life. Among his novices was the exuberant convert Fr Frederick William Faber, who soon took charge of a second Oratory in London. The relationship between the two was not a happy one and caused Newman much pain. The Oratories began to diverge on account of a tension within the Roman Catholic Church, which, in one way or another, was to absorb Newman's intellect almost to the end of his days.

This was the problem. There were forces at work in Rome determined to exalt the spiritual authority of the Pope, whose political influence was suffering decline. They found an ally among many of the converts from Anglicanism, including Cardinal Manning, who reacted against their Anglican upbringing by becoming as 'ultramontane' as they could be. Newman retained the restrained English spirit and had almost the whole of the old Catholic Church in England behind him. Some converts accused Newman of being a 'Gallican' and 'only half a Catholic'. The London Oratory, led by Fr Faber, grew ever more suspicious of Newman until eventually it arranged its own independence.

Education

For Newman the crying need in the Church was for an educated laity, yet his was a voice crying in the wilderness when he suggested it. Clericalisation and the consequent inferior position of the laity was a weakness of the Church. His bishop disagreed with him. 'He has a horror of laymen,' Newman confided. At precisely the same time, the Italian philosopher, Antonio Rosmini, was being interrogated in Rome for arguing the same thing, and his book, *The Five Wounds of the Church,* (translated by Dean Church for the Church of England) was banned. Happily, Rosmini is now rehabilitated.

It was never Newman's intention to become a theologian in the Catholic Church. He was quite content to keep his opinions to himself and get on with the work of the Oratories, which he hoped would multiply. He had no intention of writing doctrine; he thought this would be impertinent in a man who had spent most of his life outside the Catholic Church. But Newman did want to improve the education of Catholics, who by the law of the land were not allowed to graduate at Oxford and Cambridge. To this end he founded an Oratory School in 1859, from where he hoped to send his students to a University in Ireland, which he himself had founded at the request of the bishops, a Catholic University for the English-speaking world.

Sadly the University ran into difficulties. It was for laymen, and Newman expected it to be controlled by them, run not like a seminary for priests, but offering a broad-based education. In-fighting among the bishops who could not agree on its purpose kept thwarting his plans. It was opened, however, in 1854, with Newman its Rector for seven years, devoting to it his best talents and assembling a brilliant staff. Unhappily, the Government refused it a charter to grant degrees. It drew very few students from England and in 1882 what remained of it was taken into the Royal University of Ireland. At the same time as Newman was struggling with his University, and in the very year that he founded the Oratory School, he became unwittingly involved in another affair which brought right out in the open his views on the laity.

On Consulting the Faithful

The *Rambler,* an excellent literary review for Catholics, had been plunged into a crisis because its editor criticised the English Catholic bishops for remaining aloof from a Royal Commission on schools. The editor resigned, and the bishops hastily asked Newman to rescue both the periodical and their faces. Such a job appealed to him. In his first editorial on taking over he suggested that since the laity had been consulted about the definition of Mary's Immaculate Conception, the bishops would be only too glad to hear the laity's views about schools, which so concerned them. A leading Catholic theologian accused him of heresy: the laity need never be consulted about doctrinal matters.

So Newman was goaded into writing doctrine again, and in the *Rambler* published his famous article, *On Consulting the Faithful in Matters of Doctrine*. Examining the beliefs of the laity is one way of discerning the truth that has been revealed by God. The tradition of the apostles manifests itself variously at various times, 'sometimes by the mouth of the episcopacy, sometimes by the doctors, sometimes by the people.' To hammer home the point, drawing upon his earlier studies of the Arians, he asserted that in the fourth century the true faith was proclaimed far more by the faithful than by the bishops.

Some of the bishops were rendered speechless, lacking the theology to refute him – had what he said not been irrefutable. He was reported to Rome for heresy; his article, badly translated, was sent there and a list of his 'errors' was made, which Newman was never shown. Rome assumed he refused to answer the charges. The sad result was that although the matter was dropped Newman remained under suspicion in Rome for the next eight years, until two Oratorians went there and sorted the matter out.

Newman's teaching on the laity seemed outrageous to those who saw the Church primarily in juridical and institutional terms, like a club with rigid rules under the authority of the Pope. For Newman the Church was a mystical and sacramental reality in which all receive the Holy Spirit. All the faithful share in preserving and handing-on the faith. This doctrine of the Church, so long forgotten, was revived with vigour in the Second Vatican Council. The first draft of the *Constitution on the Church*, drawn up on the old lines, was rejected by the bishops as beyond amending. The one which replaced it echoes with clarity the ideas of Newman: indeed many bishops actually quoted his article in their discussions, and a new French translation of it appeared and was passed round. A whole decree on the *Apostolate of the Laity* was written. He was described as an 'unseen presence' at the Council.

His high importance in the Roman Catholic Church was stressed by Pope Paul VI during the course of the Council. No greater praise and encouragement to read him could have been uttered than this. Newman, he said,

> guided solely by the love of the truth and fidelity to Christ, traced an itinerary, the most toilsome, but also the greatest, the most meaningful, the most conclusive, that human

thought ever travelled during the last century, indeed one might say during the modern era, to arrive at the fullness of wisdom and peace.13

The First Vatican Council

Strange it is that though Newman lived through the First Vatican Council he influenced the Second more. He pleaded age and infirmity to avoid attending the First for he was glad not to go. The problems in Roman Catholicism reached their climax there, and Newman knew that forces stronger than he were at work. Ultramontanists were pressing for a definition of Papal Infallibility that would recognise virtually every Papal word as binding faith. Newman remained calm and cheerful, exchanging friendly letters with Pusey and others about it. One of these, to his bishop, sharply criticising the ultramontane clique and naming them, was made public. Newman was deeply shocked by its unlicensed publication but not sorry. He had not intended to intervene, but his views were now known.

Newman's calmness and confidence sprang from his doctrine of development, that nothing ultimately would go wrong. He was right. In the end the moderates won the day and the definition of Papal Infallibility disappointed the extremists Even so, due to the premature close of the Council the definition was set in an unfinished context, and Newman spent some time explaining this. He wrote to Miss Holmes:

13 Pope Paul VI, *Allocution on the Beatification of Dominic Barberi*, 27 October, 1963.

> We must have a little faith … The dogmas relative to the Holy Trinity and the Incarnation were not struck off all at once – but piecemeal – one Council did one thing, another a second – and so the whole dogma was built up. And the first portion of it looked extreme – and controversies rose upon it – and these controversies led to a second, and third Councils, and they did not reverse the first, but explained and completed what was first done. So it will be now. Future Popes will explain and in one sense limit their own power.[14]

Prophetically, as he envisaged, the Second Vatican Council, in its decree, the *Constitution on the Church*, did in fact set the infallibility of the Pope within the wider context of the bishops and of the whole Church, including the laity:

> The whole body of the faithful who have an anointing that comes from the Holy One cannot err in matters of belief. This characteristic is shown in the supernatural appreciation of the faith of the whole people, when 'from the bishops to the last of the faithful, they manifest a universal consent in matters of faith and morals'.[15]

Conscience

In 1874 the Prime Minister, William Gladstone, a good friend of Newman, was defeated over his Irish University Bill, and his government fell. Gladstone blamed the Irish bishops for their influence over Catholic members of Parliament, and later that year launched what he called an *Expostulation*, an attack on the Decree of Papal Infallibility, which he alleged compromised the civil liberties of Roman Catholics. Gladstone aroused much

---

14 Cited in Dessain, pp. 139-140.
15 Vatican Council II, Vol. I, ed. Austin Flannery, Dominican Publications, 1992, *Lumen Gentium*, para. 12, p. 363.

public sympathy. He wrote as though the ultramontanists had achieved their objective at the Council, requiring obedience to every word and decree of the Pope. Newman was urged to reply to this, and he did so, with some reluctance for he hated criticising others, in a long pamphlet in the form of a *Letter to the Duke of Norfolk*. He began by apologising for the ultramontanists 'who for years past have conducted themselves as if no responsibility attached to wild words and overbearing deeds … and who at length, having done their best to set the house on fire, leave to others the task of putting out the flame.' He reminded Gladstone that the Pope interfered in peoples' lives less than the State does. The *Letter* offers a nuanced explanation of Papal infallibility, and an exposition of conscience, which in all things is supreme. The Church is infallible because its revealed message is infallible and true.

> To the apostles the whole revelation was given, by the Church it is transmitted; no simply new truth has been given to us since St John's death; the one office of the Church is to guard 'that noble deposit' of truth, as St Paul speaks to Timothy, which the apostles bequeathed to her, in its fullness and integrity.[16]

The Holy Spirit guides the Church, and the Holy Spirit hinders error, but its authorities do not always obey it fully, and are not protected from the lesser consequences of human frailty.

> Was Gregory XIII (infallible) when he had a medal struck in honour of the Bartholomew massacre? or Paul IV in his

---

16 *Letter to the Duke of Norfolk*, p. 116.

conduct towards Elizabeth? or Sixtus V when he blessed the Armada? or Urban VIII when he persecuted Galileo? No Catholic ever pretends that these Popes were infallible in these acts.[17]

Catholics do not believe that 'Popes are never in the wrong and are never to be resisted.' Newman is unequivocal. 'There are extreme cases in which conscience may come into collision with the word of a Pope, and is to be followed in spite of that word.'

And his famous aphorism,

> If I am obliged to bring religion into after-dinner toasts, (which indeed does not seem quite the thing) I shall drink – to the Pope, if you please, – still, to Conscience first, and to the Pope afterwards.[18]

These words have led some to suppose that Newman was a proponent of 'loyal dissent', an advocate of 'private judgement' and a religious liberal, which could not be further from the truth. Conscience, for Newman, does not mean what people often take it to mean, a personal opinion or choice. For Newman, conscience, as Pope John Paul II explained, is not a 'sense of propriety, self-respect or good taste, formed by general culture, education and social customs.'

Newman has a very high view of conscience. It is the voice of God. This is the belief not only of Catholics, but of 'Anglicans, Wesleyans, the various Presbyterian sects in Scotland, and other denominations among us' who,

17 *Letter to the Duke of Norfolk*, p. 63.
18 *Letter to the Duke of Norfolk*, p. 66.

when they speak of conscience, 'mean what we mean, the voice of God in the nature and heart of man, as distinct from the voice of Revelation.' This inner voice of God ought never to be in conflict with the revealed Truth we receive in the Scriptures and the teaching of the Church, but rather confirm it in us. Newman recognised that this understanding of conscience is very different from that ordinarily taken of it, both by science and literature, and by the public opinion of his day.

> They do not even pretend to go by any moral rule, but they demand, what they think is an Englishman's prerogative, for each to be his own master in all things, and to profess what he pleases, asking no one's leave, and accounting priest or preacher, speaker or writer, unutterably impertinent, who dares to say a word against his going to perdition, if he like it, in his own way.[19]

> When conscience does have the right of opposing the supreme, though not infallible authority of the Pope, it must be something more than that miserable counterfeit which … now goes by the name. If in a particular case it is to be taken as a sacred and sovereign monitor, its dictate, in order to prevail against the voice of the Pope, must follow upon serious thought, prayer, and all available means of arriving at a right judgment on the matter in question … He must vanquish that mean, ungenerous, selfish, vulgar spirit of his nature, which, at the very first rumour of a command, places itself in opposition to the Superior who gives it, asks itself whether he is not exceeding his right, and rejoices, in a moral and practical matter to commence with scepticism. He must have no wilful determination to exercise a right of thinking, saying, doing just what he pleases, the question of truth and falsehood, right and wrong.[20]

---

19 *Letter to the Duke of Norfolk*, p. 58.
20 *Letter to the Duke of Norfolk*, pp. 63-64.

When Joseph Ratzinger was a student in Freising, Germany, after the war, he was very drawn to Newman's explanation of conscience. It became a fundamental foundation for *personalism*, 'which was drawing us all in its sway.' The young Joseph Ratzinger had witnessed the assertion of power that enthroned human reason without reference to God, its attempted eradication of the individual's conscience, and the way in which the German Reich had used Nietzsche's death-of-God philosophy. As Pope, he recalled it:

> We had experienced the claim of a totalitarian party, which understood itself as the fulfilment of history and which negated the conscience of the individual. One of its leaders had said: 'I have no conscience. My conscience is Adolf Hitler.' The appalling devastation of humanity that followed was before our eyes ... So it was liberating and essential for us to know that the 'we' of the Church does not rest on a cancellation of conscience, but that, exactly the opposite, it can only develop from conscience ... It was from Newman that we learned to understand the primacy of the Pope. Freedom of conscience – Newman told us – is not identical with the right 'to dispense with conscience, to ignore a Lawgiver and Judge, to be independent of unseen obligations' ... Strictly speaking, for Newman, conscience and authority could not really come into collision over matters of belief.[21]

Newman's own spiritual journey owed everything to his determination, whatever the cost, to obey his conscience.

---

21 Cardinal Joseph Ratzinger, *The Theology of Cardinal Newman*, L'Osservatore Romano, Weekly Edition in English, 1 June 2005, p. 9.

> I have always contended that obedience even to an erring conscience was the way to gain light, and that it mattered not when a man began, so that he began on what came to hand, and in faith; and that anything might become a divine method of Truth; that to the pure all things are pure, and have a self-correcting virtue and a power of germinating.[22]

For Newman, listening to the inner voice of God, conscience, is the simple and trusting conversation of prayer. It is the way to faith, the connecting principle between the creature and his Creator. People who listen to the Word within 'believe in his existence, not because others say it, not on the word of man merely, but with a personal apprehension of its truth.' Nowhere does he explain it more tenderly than in his novel, *Callista*, where he speaks through the young martyr who is asked what she means by God.

> "Well," she said, "I feel that God within my heart. I feel myself in His presence. He says to me, 'Do this: don't do that.' You may tell me that this dictate is a mere law of my nature, as is to joy or to grieve. I cannot understand this. No, it is the echo of a person speaking to me. Nothing shall persuade me that it does not ultimately proceed from a person external to me. It carries with it its proof of its divine origin. My nature feels towards it as towards a person. When I obey it, I feel a satisfaction; when I disobey, a soreness — just like that which I feel in pleasing or offending some revered friend."[23]

A Cardinal

A few days after Newman was received into the Catholic Church Dr Pusey had written in a letter to the *English Churchman:*

---

22 *Apologia*, p. 253.
23 John Henry Newman, *Callista*, Cosimo Classics, 2007, p. 244.

It is perhaps the greatest event which has happened since the communion of the Churches has been interrupted, that such an one, so formed in our Church, and the work of God's Spirit as dwelling within her, should be transplanted to theirs. If anything could open their eyes to what is good in us, or soften in us any wrong prejudices against them, it would be the presence of such an one, nurtured and grown to such ripeness in our Church, and now removed to theirs.[24]

Newman's writings, especially his *Apologia* (1864) and *Letter to the Duke of Norfolk* (1875) did bring him immediate acclaim in both Churches and in public life. His ecumenical importance lies in the fact that his journey from Anglicanism to Roman Catholicism repudiated nothing, but consisted of a long life of continual enrichment. He discovered the Catholic faith for himself, not through Roman Catholicism as such, but from his own studies of the Scriptures and the Fathers. His Anglican sermons, which influenced so many in the Church of England, he was able to re-publish as a Catholic almost unaltered, because his own studies had given him such a finely balanced appreciation of Christian truth.

It was a day of unspeakable emotion and joy in 1878 when Newman was made the first honorary Fellow of his old College, Trinity, and he returned to Oxford for the first time since 1845. He called on Pusey, and saw the new College founded in memory of Keble, and went to Littlemore too. Next year came a letter from Rome. He had been made a Cardinal, the inestimable sign of approval from the earthly head of the Church. 'The

---

24 Cited in Dessain, p. 85.

cloud is lifted from me for ever', he cried. It was while he was in Rome for the Consistory that Newman, despite his frailty, stood to deliver a remarkable discourse, which became known as the *Biglietto Speech*. So prophetic is it, so contemporary does it sound, that it is worth quoting at some length.

> For thirty, forty, fifty years I have resisted to the best of my powers the spirit of liberalism in religion... Liberalism in religion is the doctrine that there is no positive truth in religion, but that one creed is as good as another, and this is the teaching which is gaining substance and force daily. It is inconsistent with any recognition of any religion, as true. It teaches that all are to be tolerated, for all are matters of opinion. Revealed religion is not a truth, but a sentiment and a taste; not an objective fact, not miraculous; and it is the right of each individual to make it say just what strikes his fancy ... Since, then, religion is so personal a peculiarity and so private a possession, we must of necessity ignore it in the intercourse of man with man. If a man puts on a new religion every morning, what is that to you? It is as impertinent to think about a man's religion as about his sources of income or his management of his family. Religion is in no sense the bond of society.

Religious liberalism leads to the privatisation of religion, and this in turn inevitably leads to secularism. Secularism, he saw immediately, would corrode community values and destroy the inner coherence of society, which had been formed by Christianity.

> Hitherto the civil Power has been Christian. Even in countries separated from the Church, as in my own, the dictum was in force, when I was young, that: 'Christianity was the law of the land'. Now, everywhere that goodly framework of society, which is the creation of Christianity, is throwing off Christianity ... Hitherto, it has been considered that religion

alone, with its supernatural sanctions, was strong enough to secure submission of the masses of our population to law and order; now the Philosophers and Politicians are bent on satisfying this problem without the aid of Christianity. Instead of the Church's authority and teaching, they would substitute first of all a universal and a thoroughly secular education, calculated to bring home to every individual that to be orderly, industrious, and sober, is his personal interest ... As to Religion, it is a private luxury, which a man may have if he will; but which of course he must pay for, and which he must not obtrude upon others, or indulge in to their annoyance.

Infidelity is part of the reason for this state of affairs, but in England particularly it arises from the disunity of the different Christian denominations

which sprang up in England three centuries ago, and which are so powerful now, (that) have ever been fiercely opposed to the union of Church and State, and would advocate the un-Christianising of the monarchy and all that belongs to it, under the notion that such a catastrophe would make Christianity much more pure and much more powerful.

Far from making Christianity more pure and powerful it only weakens the connection between Christianity and society, and causes the subject of religion to be ignored. He goes on:

it must be borne in mind, that there is much in the liberalistic theory which is good and true; for example, not to say more, the precepts of justice, truthfulness, sobriety, self-command, benevolence, which, as I have already noted, are among its avowed principles, and the natural laws of society. It is not till we find that this array of principles is intended to supersede, to block out, religion, that we pronounce it to be evil.

He ended his speech, typically, with a paragraph of confidence and hope, grounded in his faith in the Providence of God and the indwelling and guidance of the Holy Spirit in the Church. His knowledge of Church history and the remarkable way in which the Church is renewed, led him to this conviction:

> It must not be supposed for a moment that I am afraid of it. I lament it deeply, because I foresee that it may be the ruin of many souls; but I have no fear at all that it really can do aught of serious harm to the Word of God, to Holy Church, to our Almighty King, the Lion of the tribe of Judah, Faithful and True, or to His Vicar on earth. Christianity has been too often in what seemed deadly peril, that we should fear for it any new trial now. So far is certain; on the other hand, what is uncertain, and in these great contests commonly is uncertain, and what is commonly a great surprise, when it is witnessed, is the particular mode by which, in the event, Providence rescues and saves His elect inheritance. Sometimes our enemy is turned into a friend; sometimes he is despoiled of that special virulence of evil which was so threatening; sometimes he falls to pieces of himself; sometimes he does just so much as is beneficial, and then is removed. Commonly the Church has nothing more to do than to go on in her own proper duties, in confidence and peace; to stand still and to see the salvation of God. 'The meek shall inherit the land and delight themselves in abundant peace' (Ps 37:11).[25]

Blessed are the Meek

The Beatification of John Henry Newman on 19 September 2010, and the cause of his canonisation, is, of course, the Church's recognition and celebration of his sanctity, rather than of his enormous intellect

---

25 John Henry Newman, *My Campaign in Ireland*, Aberdeen, 1896, pp. 393-400.

and library of writings, or the prodigious influence his thinking had and still has in the Church. Even during his lifetime Newman was revered, and like saints through the ages attracted 'disciples' whom he led into deeper discipleship with the Lord. John Coleridge, the Lord Chief Justice, an Anglican, said of him in 1882,

> I cannot analyse it or explain it, but to this hour he interests and awes me like no other man I ever saw. He is simple and humble as a child, and, yet, I am with a being unlike anyone else. He lifts me up for the time, and subdues me – if I said frightens me it would hardly be too strong; and yet if he does this to a commonplace old lawyer, what must it be to men who can really enter into him and feel with him.[26]

As it is with saints so it was with Newman, the secret of his influence was personal prayer, a theme that constantly occurred in his preaching, stirring up this desire in others which he had in himself. People sensed the man behind his words, and they had the witness of his life. He spent long hours in prayer every day, and kept notebooks of prayer from his Anglican days to the end of his life, praying still for the same people. He prayed for others and he prayed for himself, as his notebooks show. He prayed *for* things and *against* things. On Fridays, for instance he prayed among other things, for zeal, dependence on the grace of God, thinking of myself as an instrument, for liveliness, for a deep sense of the sacredness of the awful nature of my sacred office, for the spirit of devotion, for strength of body, nerves, voice, and breath. Asking for 'fervour' was a frequent request.

---

26 Cited in Dessain, pp. 166-7.

A prayer he wrote for his First Communion in Trinity College Chapel, when he was sixteen, he re-copied and used even as a Cardinal in the Catholic Church.

> Lord I praise Thee for calling me to the light of Thy Gospel – for my birth in a country where Thy true religion is found, and for Thy goodness in enlightening my soul with the knowledge of Thy Truth, that, whereas I was proud, self-righteous, impure, abominable, Thou wast pleased to turn me from such a state of darkness and irreligion, by a mercy which is too wonderful for me, and make me fall down humbled and abased before Thy footstool. O let me so run the race that is set before me that I may lay hold of everlasting life, and especially let me make Thee, O Holy Jesus, my pattern in my pilgrimage here, that Thou mayest be the portion of my soul to all eternity.[27]

Within the covers of this one private notebook are prayers written by a boy of sixteen, the young Anglican deacon of twenty-three, and the aged Oratorian Cardinal when he was eighty-eight, a wonderful continuity of prayer. In another notebook he used each day before Mass are the names of people he prayed for regularly, listed under headings which include Auld Lang Syne, Protestants, those dear to me, kind to me, cold to me, no how to me, godchildren, cousins, St Mary's and Littlemore, faithful women, those with claim on me, loyal to me, Catholics 1, 2 and 3, Irish friends, for the Oratory, Ecclesiastical, Converts, the Dead.

Apart from the innumerable actual prayers he wrote, his hymns and poems were also prayers, the most memorable perhaps, *Praise to the Holiest in the Height*,

---

27 Cited in Placid Murray, *Newman the Oratorian*, Gill and MacMillan, 1969, p. 60.

part of his incomparable *Dream of Gerontius*. When William Gladstone lay dying he frequently quoted this hymn, a comforting solace in his last days. Newman wrote and preached from what he experienced in the depths of his being through prayer, and people knew this. No one who has read and used the Collection of *Meditations and Devotions* that were assembled shortly after his death could doubt this for a moment. Principal Shairp, a Presbyterian Professor of Poetry, who knew him at Oxford, said of him:

> The look and bearing of the preacher were as one who dwelt apart, who, though he knew his age well did not dwell in it. From the seclusion of study and abstinence, and prayer, from habitual dwelling in the unseen, he seemed to come forth that one day of the week to speak to others of the things he had seen and known. Or, as others put it, 'He spoke as one who saw.'[28]

One who, as a boy, knew him at the Oratory, was Edward Burne-Jones, who later in life recalled Newman's influence upon him.

> When I was fifteen or sixteen he taught me so much ... things that will never be out of me. In an age of sofas and cushions he taught me to be indifferent to comfort; and in an age of materialism he taught me to venture all on the unseen ... so that if this world cannot tempt me with money and luxury, and it can't, or honours of anything else in its trumpery treasure house, it is most of all because he said it to me in a way that touched me – not scolding nor forbidding nor much leaning – walking with me a step in front.[29]

---

28 Wilfrid Ward, *The Life of John Henry Cardinal Newman* vol. 1, Longmans 1912, p. 64

29 Frances Horner, *Time Remembered*, London, 1933, p. 120.

Newman spoke frequently of holiness, and the perseverance and discipline needed to find it. Like those who heard him, as we read his words on the saints, it is difficult to escape the conclusion that, though he would never be aware of it, he was speaking of himself. The saints

> have attained such noble self-command, they have so crucified the flesh, they have so renounced the world; they are so meek, so gentle, so tender-hearted, so merciful, so sweet, so cheerful, so full of prayer, so diligent, so forgetful of injuries; they have sustained such great and continued pains, they have persevered in such vast labours, they have made such valiant confessions, they have wrought such abundant miracles, they have been blessed with such strange successes, that they have set up a standard before us of truth, of magnanimity, of holiness, of love.[30]

Newman's whole life, his purpose, his desires, his decisions, were centred on his love for Jesus Christ, and his beliefs and teaching were so grounded in the Gospel and the teachings of the apostles that their words became his own:

> What gain is it to please the world, to please the great, nay even to please those whom we love, compared with this? What gain is it to be applauded, admired, courted, followed – compared with this one aim, of not being 'disobedient to a heavenly vision'? What can this world offer comparable with that insight into spiritual things, that keen faith, that heavenly peace, that high sanctity, that everlasting righteousness, that hope of glory, which they have, who in sincerity love and follow our Lord Jesus Christ? Let us beg and pray Him day by day to reveal Himself to our souls more fully, to quicken our

---

30 John Henry Newman, *Discourses Addressed to Mixed Congregations*, Longmans, Green, and Co., 1906, p. 101

senses, to give us sight and hearing, taste and touch of the world to come; so to work within us, that we may sincerely say, 'Thou shall guide me with Thy counsel, and after that receive me with glory. Whom have I in heaven but Thee? and there is none upon earth that I desire in comparison of Thee. My flesh and my heart faileth, but God is the strength of my heart, and my portion for ever.'[31]

He gave his soul back to God on 11 August 1890 in his ninetieth year. He had lived eleven years since being made a Cardinal, years that he continued to devote to praying, writing, and in leading his growing community and thriving school, keeping up, as ever, with his correspondence and meeting all who came to see him. They were years of contentment, free from the setbacks, controversies and misunderstandings, which had, for him, been a means of grace, born without complaint. The Oratory was filled for his Requiem Mass with Bishops, hundreds of Catholic clergy and dignitaries, his pupils from the Oratory School, the Duke of Norfolk, the Lord Chief Justice, Anglican clergy and Oxford dons. And more than 15,000 people lined the route as his body was carried from the Oratory to Rednal, where one of England's greatest sons was laid to rest.

31 John Henry Newman, *Parochial and Plain Sermons*, vol. VIII, Longmans, Green, and Co., p. 32.

TWO PRAYERS OF CARDINAL NEWMAN

1. May He support us all the day long,
    till the shades lengthen and the evening comes,
    and the busy world is hushed,
    and the fever of life is over,
    and our work is done.
    Then in His mercy may He give us a safe lodging,
    and a holy rest and peace at the last.

2. God has created me to do Him some definite service;
    He has committed some work to me,
    which He has not committed to another.
    I have my mission – I may never know it in this life,
    but I shall be told it in the next … .
    I am a link in a chain, a bond of connection between
        persons.
    He has not created me for naught. I shall do good, I shall do
        His work;
    I shall be an angel of peace, a preacher of truth in my own
        place, while not intending it,
    if I do but keep His commandments and serve Him in my
        calling.

    Therefore I will trust Him.
    Whatever, wherever I am, I can never be thrown away.
    If I am in sickness, my sickness may serve Him;
    In perplexity, my perplexity may serve Him;
    If I am in sorrow, my sorrow may serve Him …
    He may prolong my life, he may shorten it;
    He knows what He is about.
    He may take away my friends;
    He may throw me among strangers,
    He may make me feel desolate, make my spirits sink
    Hide the future from me – still He knows what he is about.

    O Adonai, O Ruler of Israel,
    Thou that guidest Joseph like a flock,
    O Emmanuel, O Sapientia,
    I give myself to Thee. I trust Thee wholly.
    Thou art wiser than I – more loving than I myself.

Deign to fulfil Thy high purposes in me whatever they be –
   work in and through me.
I am born to serve Thee, to be Thy instrument.
Let me be Thy blind instrument.
I ask not to see – ask not to know – I ask simply to be used.